# RENEE McGEE WHITLEY

❖

# GIVE ME THIS MOUNTAIN

*The Little* Biblically Based *Real Estate Book*

This publication is the sole possession of

# Renee Mcgee Whitley

Library of Congress

Copyright Case # 1-199423361
ISBN 978-1-61623-767-7

GIVE ME THIS MOUNTAIN
(*Revised*)

Author's Photograph
William H. Whitley, Jr.
(Photo Tres Bien of Baton Rouge, LA)

Edited by
Paulette L. Grey
Patricia Ann Grissett
Franchesca Rebecca Williams

---

**Disclaimer**

The information contained in this book is subject to the rules and laws that govern real estate from state to state. Real estate information is subject to change. Be sure to consult your local real estate broker and/or mortgage officer in the event rules, laws, and practices have changed or vary from those outlined in this book.

# Table of Contents

# Acknowledgements

For my husband, William, and the additional love for four plus three.

For my children- Jeremiah, Marguerita, Paulette, and Jonathan –
who have got to have a better day.

For my sisters and brother: Patricia, Debra, Boaz, Sandra, and Renita;
our children, and our children's children.

For women who have been true friends:
Gloria Trotter, Shirley Wright, Tracy Sheppard, Yolanda Wright.

For those clients who provided the transportation (Ms. Alberta)
to show them *their* properties of interest.
Wonderful you, thank you for allowing me to be your REALTOR.
Your business caused me to sell a million dollars worth of property
my first year as a full time real estate agent—
and I did not even have a car!

For the customers to whom I have already sold property
and hope will call on me again.

For Chrystal Lathan and Charlotte Guidroz, loan officers
who continued working with me even though I was extremely
demanding, because they knew I was about "myyyyyyyyy" people,
about my all-important clients, about **Y-O-U**.

For real estate seekers, especially those who are trying to purchase
their very first home, because I know there are times when it is
difficult to get the assistance you need when your dollars aren't big.

For single women and single parents who press everyday, all day,
to take care of and provide for their children.

*Absent from the body, but ever present...*
For my mom, Marguerite Johnson McGee Hibbler,
and the steps she took to love and protect her seven babies.
You are ever with me.

For my oldest sister, Margaret "Jean," who told me and showed me it
was important to "make my own tracks."

For Auntie Irene, who would not support my attempts to feel justified
in thoughts of giving up when things got really rough.

---

*"And ye shall know the truth, and the truth shall make you free."*
*John 8:32*

*"...and with all thy getting, get an understanding."*
*Proverbs 4:7*

*"...The Lord commanded Moses to give us an inheritance among our brethren..."*
*Joshua 17:4*

*"Beloved, I wish above all things that thou mayest prosper and be in health, even as
thy soul prospereth."*
*3 John 2*

---

Yours for the Cause of Calvary,

Renee

# Dedication

*This book is dedicated to my mother,*
**Marguerite Johnson McGee Hibbler,**
*who taught me that loving God, my children,*
*and knowledge,*
*along with living with perseverance,*
*are the keys to obtaining all my desires.*

*I will always love you, Momma.*

**"Nellie"**

# Preface

The purpose of this book is to provide you with assistance through the sometimes confusing, overwhelming, and what may seem harsh world of qualifying for property ownership.

This book does not pretend to provide all the answers. Digest what you can and disregard what you wish, but above all -

# GET
# YOUR
# MOUNTAIN!

Renee McGee Whitley

## Chapter One
## YOUR INHERITANCE

"The Lord commanded Moses to give us an inheritance among our brethren..." (Joshua 17:4).

Joshua 17:4 is the foundational scripture for this book. It is also the inspiration for the title of this book, and I believe this scripture establishes the precept that all of mankind has a right to possess the land. So let us move forward by first taking a look backward, back to the beginning.

It is my belief that the best place to begin anything is at the beginning. So let us go back, back to the beginning of time, back to where there was no sky, no sea, no land, no mountains, no birds, nothing—except God. In that beginning, God created all we see, and according to Genesis 1:26, HE (God) left all of

His creation to mankind. God himself did this and HE (God) did so by putting it this way:

> "And God said, Let us make man in our image, after our likeness: and let them have dominion over the fish of the sea, and over the fowl of the air, and over the cattle, and over all the earth, and over every creeping thing that creepeth upon the earth."

God gave man "dominion" over the earth and all that is upon the earth! In order to truly understand the significance of this scripture, we must first define the word "dominion."

> VINES DICTIONARY
> **Dominion** (n) - Denotes lordship (Kuriotes), whether angelic or human, over something physical (in this case, God's creation: the earth, sea, sky, and animals)

> WEBSTER'S DICTIONARY
> **Dominion** (n) - 1. rule; power 2. governed territory

According to Genesis 1:26, God, after making all the earth and all its contents, made man and gave him [man or mankind] authority, ownership, rulership over it. Can you truly fathom what this means? God created you, mankind, with a built-in inheritance! And that inheritance is God's earth. You have the right to posses and to occupy a portion of this earth. Y-O-U have a right to property ownership!

It does not matter your color, size, shape, education level, or the demographic area from which you come or currently live. Neither your ethnicity, social and economic level, **nor anything else aborts this inheritance.** You, mankind, were created with this built-in, automatic inheritance from the day of your inception. Even the poorest of the poor are birthed with a dowry, and it comes directly from God to Y-O-U! Is that not completely awesome?

Try to wrap your mind around this truth: God's word is immutable. That means it cannot be changed. God's word can never be made ineffective, nor can it be stopped. Say it with me: "God's word is immutable!"

*Immutable – The inability to alter!*

I know that some of you may find this difficult to believe. However, it is true! Maybe you are a person who needs proof, and for some reason this biblical verse is just not enough evidence for you. The scriptures recognize this possibility when speaking of the witness of two. Matthew 18:19, when paraphrased, states that the witness or testimony of two is a powerful, trustable witness.

When speaking of something that is verifiable, the Holy Scriptures speak about two sources confirming the same thing. It is written this way: "**...in the mouth of two or three witnesses every word may be established**" (Matthew 18:16).

John 8:17 further attests of the surety that rests in the identical testimony of two or more sources. The apostle John records this: "**It is also written in your law, that the testimony of two men is true.**" Two scriptures written by two different men (apostles) concur. This wonderful biblical authority is here for you and me and continues to exist today, right now!

Do you need more? Is the Bible not enough for you? Perhaps the United States

Government provides the second source of testimony, further evidence of your inherent right to own property. The last clause of the **Fifth Amendment to the United States Constitution guarantees all Americans the right to own private property.** The fifth line of the Fifth Amendment states that even if one is a criminal, such an individual shall not be deprived of property. This statement therefore recognizes any individual's right to own property, one of our nation's basic freedoms. Our entire capitalistic system is based on a right to equality.

There you have it, a second source for the same evidence. God's Word and the United States Constitution attest to the same fact. **You have the right to property ownership!**

Yes, you who say:

"But I have no money."

"I have no connections."

"My credit is not so good."

"My parents won't help me."

"My student loan is in default."

"I don't know how to obtain a loan…"

These statements—and every other statement contrary to what God's Word says about you—must yield to the truth. The truth is that you can own your own home. I cannot say this enough, nor can I over emphasize this wonderful truth. You can own your own home. You can, you can, and again, yes you can! Now you say it: "Yes I can! Yes I Can!"

*Annie Get Your Gun* is one of my favorite movies. In this movie, Annie is a sharp shooting cowgirl. She is in love with a handsome cowboy who, like her, is a sharp shooter that travels around the region in rodeo shows. The problem is that her love interest tries to tell her what she can and cannot do. In love, but not to be daunted, Annie declares, "YES I CAN, YES I CAN, YES I CAN-CAN!"

Now if Annie Oakley, a fictitious character in a fictitious movie, can declare her competencies, (competencies based solely on her confidence in her own abilities), surely the believing Y-O-U can declare your rights based on the Word of God and our U.S. Constitution.

In order to truly grasp this truth, however, your focus must be on learning. You must also focus on changing certain problems that may stand between you and home ownership. You do this by equipping yourself with the right information.

You must not focus on your fears. It is fear of what I call the *giants* and seeing them as impossible foes that will cause you not to enter into the promises of "reignship" and "*giant* slaying" mentality. I call *giants* those obstacles, (some real and some imagined), that stand in your path to block you from your goal of property ownership.

Just like the children of Israel saw a nation of giants, which seemed impossible to defeat (but were indeed defeated), you too, must arm yourself with the right battling tools. Instead of fearing, avoiding, or agreeing with the *giants*, do what it takes to overcome them.

Anything built is only as strong as its foundation. Therefore, this book will dedicate time to how you can strengthen your foundation of faith and realize your dream of owning your own home.

The next chapter focuses on identifying the *giants*, those obstacles that stand between you and home ownership. The purpose of Chapter Two is to equip you with the ability to recognize your own *giants*. Whether real or imagined, self-induced or the result of being unfairly victimized, know that the *giants* in your life are absolutely defeatable.

# *GIANTS* STANDING IN THE WAY

In this chapter you will read about seven different issues that often interfere with the ability to possess the promise of inheritance. Here, the specific topic is home ownership. Perhaps you will find your foe in more than one category.

The intent of this section is not to attack you. It is the job of the enemy to blame, accuse, and attack. The purpose of knowledge and accurate information is to direct you, to be a guiding light so that you can walk without stumbling. This book is written to be that light. Remember this book is not about blaming you; it is instead about liberating you. Dare to read on. Dare to face your *giants*, no matter how big they are!

Let me begin by first asking where you are in your belief system. Do you believe it when I say that you, too, can be a property owner? Do you believe the expert witnesses I have cited? Or are you so focused on the following: unacceptable credit history ("poor credit score"), inconsistent work record, unemployment, lack of sufficient cash, fear of rejection, generational curses of poverty, low self-esteem, corporate prejudice, fear of the paperwork, and so on?

If you see these circumstances as insurmountable obstacles, then you are not looking at the truth! It does not matter what your particular *giant* is called. Just like Goliath, there is a rock that will knock your *giant* out! The point I am trying to make is that no problem is insurmountable. All of your *giants* can be reckoned with. All of them can be defeated. All of them can be "knocked out," never to rise and do battle with you again.

What you see may be real, just as the twelve spies saw real *giants*. The facts are present, but there is a truth that moves beyond even facts. The truth is what has been said time and time again: YOU CAN OWN YOUR HOME! If you are focusing solely on the problem, then your focus is on what could be a very temporary situation. These barriers—what I call the *giants*—will come down, but it is up to you to knock them down.

## *Giant* Number 1 – Poor Credit

It is unfortunate that many people do not learn about credit until they discover that their own is inadequate. Sadly, they discover it right when wanting to purchase that perfect car, an all-important appliance, or their dream home.

**Just as weak or poor credit does not just happen, neither will rising out of it.** This *giant* may have been sown when you first entered college, when suddenly you were given that mystical credit card! Suddenly you were able to go to the mall and charge, charge, charge—not knowing that something called a "credit history" was being created on little, unsuspecting you. It never occurred to you that paying the bill by a certain time was all that important.

Maybe you just had to have that bad-to-the-bone outfit, and realizing that you did not have enough cash to pay for it, you simply whipped out your wonderful I'm-an-adult credit card; and yes, you charged it. You even qualified for student loans and accepted the maximum funds allotted, paying for not only the classes and books, but also all the other niceties you deserved.

It is easy to see just how quickly debt can accrue. Now, old debts (some you have completely forgotten about) are standing between you and your desire for home ownership. Applying with lender after lender, you are now told that your credit score is unacceptable.

Do not despair. Unacceptable credit can be repaired. Chapter Three will address this foe and set you on your new path to restoration!

## *Giant* Number 2 - Inconsistent Employment

You now have a wonderful job making adequate money, and you want to purchase your dream home. There is, however, a problem. The mortgage company informs you that your work history is inadequate and they cannot give you a home loan. How could the lenders be so cruel?

Perhaps you do not have two years of uninterrupted employment. Perhaps before securing your present job, you were unemployed for several months. Maybe you were fired because you just could not get along with your supervisor or coworkers. Perhaps you recently graduated from school and obtained a job in your field, but all of your past employment is scanty, to say the least.

Does your work history look like a checkerboard? Have you changed jobs often, never working at one place for a full two years? Do you have gaps in your employment history?

Whatever your exact situation, you now have the *giant* of inconsistent employment standing between you and your dream home. There is a way to defeat this very real and all too intimidating *giant*!

# *Giant* Number 3 -
# The Fallacy of Money Trees
## (High Debt-To-Income Ratio)

Money does not grow on trees. Even if you have a great job and enjoy a comfortable income, it is not a good idea to amass a lot of debt. Contrary to what you may believe, it is not enough to simply pay your bills on time, especially your credit card bills.

While your credit card company may delight in you repeatedly using your charge card(s) and faithfully making the required <u>minimum</u> monthly payment, paying only the minimum balance is not necessarily a wise practice. Your credit score may not actually suffer from such a practice, but your goal should be to decrease, limit, and, if possible, eliminate debt.

The best use of a credit card is to pay more than the minimum balance, ideally paying the entire balance within 30 days of making the charge. No matter how faithfully you make your minimum monthly payments, your credit worthiness could be negatively impacted when you carry the charged balance past 30 days.

After this 30-day period, you have begun what is called revolving credit. Your credit card company is now earning three, four, five times or more above the actual cost of the purchased item. This *giant* must be slain immediately.

Example:  You purchase a pair of shoes for $75.00 with your charge card that has an 18% rate. Each time you make your minimum payment of $19.00, only $5.50 is actually going toward the debt, while the other $13.50 is being paid as interest to the credit card company. In this example, it will take 13.6 months to actually pay off this $75.00.

$19.00 x 13.6 months = $258.40 you will pay for a $75.00 pair of shoes! Let's not forget to add the cost of 13 stamps @ $.49 per stamp, and an additional $6.37 has been spent for **a total of $264.77 for a $75.00 pair of shoes!**

If you can see your spending practices in the example on the previous page, then you are spending your money as if it grows on trees.

Computerized programs are designed to score credit accounts that carry balances over a 30-day period less positively than accounts in which balances are paid off within a 30-day period. At times, creditors frown on purchases that carry a balance over 30 days (when the debt-to-income ratio is high) because it appears that the individual is living off the credit card. This sends the message that the individual's income is not ample enough to cover his or her debts and would therefore make him or her an unlikely candidate for a mortgage loan.

**You should also know that having a large amount of debt might be as bad for your credit as debt that is carried over a long time.** Even if you pay your bills on time, having a lot of debt can lower your credit score. If you owe more than 30% to 40% of your gross monthly income in long-term debt, you could be denied a home loan.

Are you guilty of spending your money as if it grows on trees? Clear signs that you may be under the influence of the "Money Trees" *giant*:

- Uncontrollable or impulse spending
- Failure to adhere to your budget
- Large debt load
- Credit cards consistently maxed out
- Overly stuffed closets and drawers (with things you do not even use)
- Feelings of guilt after purchases
- Constant juggling of funds

Be sure to read Chapter Three for how to defeat this *giant*. He, too, can be defeated!

## *Giant* Number 4 – No Cookies in the Cookie Jar

This is perhaps the most common and dominant *giant* of them all. Simply having little to no money left over for savings after you pay your monthly obligations becomes the norm rather than the unusual. Do not be discouraged. Even this *giant* can be addressed and removed as a hindrance on your road to home ownership.

Is this *giant* operating in your life because you must have a new outfit or get your hair done every week? Maybe your need for cable, the latest cellular phone, a designer purse, or eating out is the reason this *giant* so boldly reigns over you.

This "No Cookies in the Cookie Jar" *giant* masquerades himself as harmless, as he whispers to your hungry ears: "You deserve it…Go ahead…Tomorrow is not promised…If you don't treat yourself nobody else will…"

All of these statements seem harmless enough, but when this is used as a rationale to "spend, spend, spend" to the point where you have no money between paychecks, then you are a victim of the "No Cookie" *giant*.

This *giant* works in an addictive nature, giving you an adrenaline rush every time you spend. If you find yourself shopping when you are depressed, under stress, feel insecure or just plain bored, then it is a possibility that this ole *giant* is at work.

The scriptures give a stern warning about placing our affections where they should not be. Like Samson who laid his head in Delilah's lap (Judges Chapter 16), you will not find lasting comfort and enjoyment in over spending.

If you find yourself sneaking your purchases in the house, then the "No Cookies in the Cookie Jar" *giant* is hard at work. If you lie to your partner about how much money you have really spent, you may be out of control with your spending.

Is reckless spending worth the possibility of destroying your marriage? Is it worth paying rent on someone else's property for the rest of your life? Surely, you agree that it is not. That is why you are reading this book. Please be sure to read Chapter Three to find out what weapons to use to annihilate this enemy.

## *Giant* Number 5 –
## 007 Syndrome

Is your *giant* what I like to call the "007 Syndrome?" This particular *giant* welds his strength by keeping you so busy maintaining your privacy that you are too secretive to let anyone know your business. If you ever apply for a mortgage, you are definitely going to have to give someone your "top secret" information.

If you are so private that you will not allow yourself to ask for help or seek answers which may aide you in mastering better spending practices, then it just may cost you better credit scores and interest rates. If this is Y-O-U, then the "007" *giant* stands boldly in your way!

Do you suspect a conspiracy in everything? Do you believe everyone is out to get you? Are you running from responsibility, seeing it as a yoke you must not be entangled with? Are you battling a fear of entering into the long-term commitment a mortgage requires? Do you rationalize your moving from apartment to apartment, with the excuse that you just do not trust "that" mortgage company? Have you visited house after house, gone from one real estate agent to another, dancing with many, but faithful to no one?

If you find truth in any of the above, the "007 Syndrome" *giant* is at work. This *giant* is always battling, always running, desperately trying to escape from one enemy or another. Perhaps you, too, are hiding, running, battling an enemy that can only be uncovered if you would look intently in the mirror. The truth: **Everyone is not out to get you.**

The "007 Syndrome" *giant* is as dangerous as the James Bond character. This *giant* leaves you forever functioning on the outside, over the limits and living at risk. Such practices keep you forever moving, never settling into anything. If this is you, then it is time you let the "007 Syndrome" go!

## *Giant* Number 6 – Mr. and Ms. Know It All

Perhaps your particular *giant* is the inability to ask questions and seek help because **you feel that you already know e-e-e-e-e-verything.** Are you the person who always has to lead or be the head of EVERYTHING, even when someone who is more skilled is available?

"Mr. and Ms. Know It All" get a large portion of their information from the "grapevine." You know what was said but cannot remember where you heard it; still, you stake your life on it being true.

Is the reason you do not own your own home because you "heard" the mortgage rates would be better in the nebulous future of some other distant time? Maybe you located the perfect house, but a cousin of your best friend's husband told you a re-zoning is about to occur, or that an apartment complex will be coming up just across the street from that wonderful house. Never mind that you did not go to the city planning office to seek **factual** information.

**Are you the person who can take no one's advice, but you always insist on giving yours?** You think you know it all, but you actually have the least of all. The "Know It All" *giant's* closet friend is pride.

We all know that **"pride goeth before destruction..."** (Proverbs 16:18). Do not let the *giant* of "I Know Everything" continue to lead you down the wrong road, the road of misinformation.

Do you truly believe that no one can add anything to you? Surely you do not. You may feel that you are self-sufficient, but without even the trees and plants you and I could not live. We need oxygen! We all need something and someone, and that is okay.

> "A man's pride shall bring him low: but honor shall uphold the humble in spirit" (Proverbs 29:23).

# *Giant* Number 7 – Bankruptcy

**Do not be mistaken. Filing bankruptcy does not necessarily relinquish you from all your debts.** It may be that due to circumstances beyond your control or past behaviors of poor discipline, you chose to file for a bankruptcy, believing it would relieve you from all your debts and stress.

Situations such as illness, family crisis, or divorce may be reasons you opted for bankruptcy. Perhaps you were informed that bankruptcy was the easiest way to end financial stress. Thinking that you had no other option, you filed for bankruptcy.

Now with a bankruptcy on your credit report, you discover that you were misinformed. You still have credit obligations. Everything was **not** discharged from your debt history. Coupled with this, you are not credit worthy. If you do obtain credit, you find yourself in a perpetual deadlock of absurdly high interest. Now you feel more stress than ever.

Bankruptcy may have a long reach into your future, leaving you feeling desperate, hopeless, and ashamed, or functioning as a misfit Siamese twin to the "007 Syndrome." You may have fallen off your financial horse, but do not shoot the animal just yet!

Bankruptcy is not the end. A new beginning can be around the next bend. You, however, are the only one who can decide this. You are reading this book for a reason. You desire a new start, a home of your own. You are on the right track. Facing your battles is the beginning. The "Bankruptcy" *giant* can be conquered!

Now that a few of the obstacles, the *giants* that you may face, have been duly exposed, Chapter Three will focus on defeating them. Yes, you can defeat these once believed insurmountable obstacles. Please read on and make notes; and if necessary, reread Chapter Three again and again. If this sounds like too much work, just remember that your dream of home ownership is worth it.

# Now that the *giants* have been exposed, use the space below to write a personal prayer for strength and clarity in facing them.

_____

_____

_____

_____

_____

_____

_____

_____

_____

_____

_____

_____

_____

_____

"For now we see through a glass, darkly, but then face to face: now I know in part; but then shall I know even as also I am known" (1 Corinthians 13:12).

# Chapter Three
# DEFEATING YOUR *GIANTS*

I know it may seem impossible. You must, however, believe that getting rid of the *giants* that stand in your way is no more impossible than those that the twelve spies of Israel faced and defeated as they spied out the "promised land" (Numbers 13:17-33).

Like ten of the twelve spies who went to examine the "promised land," you may have your eyes so full of the obstacles that you cannot even focus on the promise. Nevertheless, two of the twelve men believed that they could possess the land, despite what seemed impossible odds. They believed in the promise, the Giver of that promise, and their right to occupy the "promised land!"

In Numbers 14:1-9, the children of Israel faced an enemy that seemed impossible to defeat. The exhortation they received was to –

### 1) STOP FEARING (Numbers 14:9)

Before any obstacle you face can be reckoned with, you must first stop seeing it as an impossible foe, as one that cannot be defeated. In other words, stop fearing the situation. Normally fear leads to intimidation, which often causes an individual to avoid dealing with the source of the fear. All too often, when fear sets in, we have the tendency to behave as if the problem does not exist, to run from the issue or cover the fear by masking it with other things.

**Please hear me. You cannot simply ignore a poor credit record or unstable employment record and think it will simply go away on its own!**

The biblical history of Numbers 14 records a story about two men whose names were Joshua and Caleb. Only Joshua and Caleb encouraged the children of Israel to believe that God would enable them to take the land. Only Joshua and Caleb exhorted the others to trust God. To paraphrase their words: If God is pleased with us, HE will see us through. This scripture leads me to the second point concerning facing and defeating your *giants* –

### 2) OPERATE IN HONESTY

## Defeating *Giant* Number 1 – Poor Credit

While the scriptures are always true, they are not to be used out of context. This is not the time to implement the scripture: **"...forgetting those things which are behind..."** (Philippians 3:13). Far too often, many otherwise honest people are willing to live dishonestly when it comes to debt. If you truly see yourself as upright, then pay what you owe.

**This will require that you arm yourself with integrity, patience, perseverance, and honesty.** Neither God nor man can possibly take delight in a dishonest person. It is my belief that instead of running from a past due bill and waiting for it to simply disappear from your credit report, Y-O-U must face your *giant*.

Here are the steps to do so:

Step 1:   **Get a current copy of your credit report.** If you have recently been denied credit, you may obtain a free credit report by contacting the credit bureaus—Experian, Transunion, or Equifax—providing the name of the company that denied you credit.

Step 2:   **Review the credit report, and then acknowledge the debt you created.** If debts that do not belong to you are found in your credit report, write a letter to the credit bureaus denying the debts. An investigation will then ensue.

Step 3:   **Contact the creditors listed in your credit report.**

Step 4:    Talk to the creditors about your desire to pay
           off the debt.

Step 5:    Work out a reasonable plan to pay the debt.

**It is a must that you consistently and faithfully work the plan of paying YOUR debt.** There are times when creditors will delete hundreds (if not thousands) of dollars in interest and late fees (which have in many instances been attached to delinquent debts), if the individual would simply contact the creditor and offer an acceptable payment plan. It is imperative that you stick to the plan you make by paying the money you agree to pay in the exact time you said you would pay.

*If some unforeseen misfortune arises that prevents you from making a payment on time, you should contact the creditor immediately.* Communicate the problem and quickly resume the original payment plan. (If possible, pay a bit more to catch up where you fell behind.) Once a lender has had an opportunity to observe your good word (which is established by your consistency in payments), you will usually find a willing (if not anxious) individual who is more than ready to work with you in ways which demonstrate the favor of God.

I can almost hear some of you saying:

"I don't have a large amount of money for a down payment..."

"I don't have enough money to pay off all my past due credit obligations..."

"I just began work on this good job, and I just didn't know how important credit was when I started out. That's how I got such a poor credit history..."

"I don't really owe anyone from past due delinquencies. It's just that all of my credit history shows I've always paid late..."

"I have no credit at all, good or bad, and everyone wants to see credit, good credit..."

All of these issues are valid, but none of them are impossible to conquer. **Most banks and**

## credit unions will aid you in rebuilding credit by providing you a "secured loan."

Example: Your request is to borrow $500 and pay the funds back over one year. To aid you in reestablishing credit, your loan request is granted, provided you place the same amount in your account as "frozen." This means you cannot access the $500 in your personal account. As you make your monthly payment on the $500, each month that same amount is "unfrozen" on your money. If you faithfully make your payments each month, you have established one perfect account, and in so doing, pulled up your credit score.

A secured loan is an excellent way to reestablish credit. If you wish, you do not have to spend a full year repaying on such a loan. Be sure, however, that you do not pay the debt off before six months. In order for a creditor to report a history on you, you must pay the creditor a minimum of six months. Anything shorter than this does not get reported to the credit bureau. Therefore, even if an account is paid perfectly, any payment less than six months will not raise your credit score.

**Remember, the credit line on a secured loan must be at least six months to be reported to the credit bureau.**

As you demonstrate your ability to honor credit lines, you increase your credit worthiness. Eventually you will be able to acquire an unsecured loan. Obtaining a "secured" loan is a safe way to rebuild credit quickly.

Adding your name to the account or credit card of a parent or spouse (who is in excellent credit standing) is another way to improve your credit score. In so doing, you, too, can share in that wonderful rating. This is a great way to quickly improve one's credit standing. You do not even need to actually use the credit card or have access to the account; and it is perfectly legal!

Remember, most lenders are looking for as little as three good credit lines—along with having all past due accounts satisfied, proof of ample income, and adequate employment— before providing you with a mortgage loan. You do not have to extend credit beyond a six-month period if your intention is to establish good credit and avoid being in long-term and unnecessary debt.

As you pay off old debt, you must work to establish a <u>new</u> record that demonstrates your ability to pay your obligations in a timely manner. Your name is tied to a history! It speaks volumes about you!

> "A good name is rather to be chosen than great riches, and loving favour rather than silver and gold" (Proverbs 22:1).

Creditors are not expecting you to be perfect at all times. What they do expect, however, is evidence of consistency and reliability. When applying for a mortgage, it is that evidence of paying your debts on time that is most critical. Y-O-U **can do it!**

## Defeating *Giant* Number 2 – Inconsistent Employment

This *giant* can often be a two-headed monster of pride and laziness. While the economy is often to blame for job loss, it is not the sole reason for all who are unemployed. This may be an unpopular and perhaps menacing area.

As you read, however, try to remember that the objective is to free yourself, ultimately achieving your goal of home ownership. In order to truly release direction and provide assistance, even the difficult must be faced.

Today, perhaps as in no other time, *image* has become a humongous deal. The logo of jeans, shoes, purses, and even cell phones are accepted as symbols that one has "arrived." Never mind if you have a Cadillac while living in a low-income housing unit. So what if your name is tied to a horrible credit history. You have a Gucci bag. Never mind that the wallet inside the Gucci bag is empty!

If you are to be delivered, you must first live in reality. **There is no shame in honest work.** If you happen to have an inconsistent employment history due to illness, disability, or serious changes in your life, this is understandable. Expect a breakthrough and be encouraged.

For those, however, who are unemployed or under-employed simply because of pride and/or laziness, it time to GET UP! Consider the ants, and get up! (Please read Proverbs 6:6.) If you want the best, you must give the best.

You must do the following in order to have a home of your own:

**Secure a permanent job, and work the job faithfully.**
- If currently self-employed, a minimum of three years, proof with a 1099, and income tax returns are required when applying for a home mortgage.
- If employed with two years of work, provide proof with income tax returns and W2s.

**Keep your debt within reason.**
- Long-term debt* should not exceed 30% to 40% of your gross monthly income.
- You must have ample income to cover the mortgage of the home.

**You must pay your debts on time.**
- Maintain three to four lines of credit with acceptable credit/payment history.
- Any previous delinquent credit must be rectified to a zero balance.

*Long-term debt* – Any financed obligation or bill that will require an excess of 10 months to satisfy to a zero balance.

I hope that you were not expecting some magic wand, cure-all answer. The answer only takes Y-O-U making up your mind. Your mind must be made up to go to work and stay on your job.

The focus on home ownership—remembering that there is honor in honest work—should be motivation enough. If you have to mop the floor, mop it well. If you have to bag groceries, bag them with a smile—with a mental picture of yourself sitting in your **own** den (when you leave work)!

Now knock the *giant* of unemployment out by going to work and staying on that job until you locate a better one. Do not allow laziness to cause you to create excuses and selfish reliance on others. Do not allow foolish pride to keep you from doing a job others may deem menial. Your objective is to acquire income through legal employment.

Avoid those who do not mirror your goals and efforts. Pray for strength, new habits, and motivation. Because it is an honorable request, you will receive it. Y-O-U decide whether the *giants* will be defeated in your life!

## Defeating *Giant* Number 3 – The Fallacy of Money Trees
### and
## Defeating *Giant* Number 4 – No Cookies in the Cookie Jar

Surely if today's economy does not bear witness that money does not grow on trees, then I do not know what does. Someone wise once said that desperate times call for desperate measures.

There is a scripture: **"To every thing there is a season, and a time to every purpose under the heaven"** (Ecclesiastes 3:1). This scripture speaks of discerning the times.

Since you are reading this book, you understand that it is time to be free. You are ready to move from simply acquiring knowledge to utilization of that knowledge. You understand that in order for savings to increase, spending must decrease. Knowing that your desire is to own your own home, saving (rather than spending) must become your focus.

The Book of Wisdom states: **"Wisdom is the principal thing; therefore get wisdom: and with all thy getting get an understanding"** (Proverbs 4:7).

Here is the wisdom:  Having and using a charge card can actually be beneficial.  When used wisely, a charge card can have added value or benefits.  Some charge cards offer rewards or bonus points, but they also come with strict penalties.

If you have a credit card, be sure you understand the terms and use it in ways that benefit you.  It is also a wise practice to use your charge cards primarily for one-time purchases such as appliances, furniture, annual trips, etc.  Avoid using your charge card for recurring purchases such as clothing and groceries, unless you are going to pay the balance off within 30 days.

You now understand that spending every penny you make is not a wise practice. Money does not grow on trees. Defeating the "Money Tree" and "Empty Cookie Jar" *giants* in your life requires a plan.

Here are the steps:

Step 1:  **Start by paying yourself.*** By saving ten to fifteen percent of your increase, you are paying yourself increase. (If you cannot save this amount, just be sure you begin to save something <u>consistently</u>.) Place this money in a facility that is in an inconvenient location, and do not get an ATM card connected to this savings account. This will make it at least inconvenient for you to draw the money out. (You can also talk to experts about investing.)

*Paying one's tithes and offering, of course, supersedes everything—including paying yourself via savings and investment accounts (Malachi 3:10-12).

Step 2:  **Stay out of the shopping centers.** In all likelihood, you have plenty of clothes and shoes. If you do happen to go to a shopping center with a friend or perhaps to pick up something for your child, take only the money you have budgeted to spend. If you see something you think you want to purchase, but the item is not in your budget, do not buy it at that time. Instead, ask the cashier to "hold" it for you. Statistics show that 80% of the items put on hold are never purchased.

**Step 3:** **Shop with cash only.** When you shop with cash you see the physical money leaving your hand. Therefore you are more cognizant of exactly how much you are actually spending.

**Step 4:** **Review your plan often.** Keep your goals of having good credit and home ownership fresh in your mind. Use some of your free time to drive through desired neighborhoods, and discuss your plans with your circle of support.

Remember, you must stop the impulse shopping. Even window-shopping with a friend might be a bad idea for you. You are in the recovery phase so you do not need to tempt your will. If you do happen to go to a shop, do not take money that is planned for something else. Shopping with credit cards is a no-no. Your surplus money for your savings will come as you exercise self-control.

## Two *giants* down with one smooth stone: Discipline is its name!

# Defeating *Giant* Number 5 – 007 Syndrome

It is not healthy to live your life disconnected because you have difficulty trusting everyone. You need to recognize this, too, is an enemy and slay it by letting nothing stop you from getting the information you need. Of course, you should be careful that you are dealing with legitimate, reliable, and reputable people.

Are you worthy of trust? If you are, believe that other people are also. Get rid of the distrustful attitude, and get real.

Stop now and take off the dark glasses, Maxwell Smart. (You remember Maxwell Smart on the show "Get Smart." He was a clumsy secret agent who always fouled things up.) As long as you are paying rent, you are paying for another person's property. "The Man" you believe that is out to get you can be seen every time you look in the mirror. His name is fear, and he is a companion of procrastination and distrust.

Consider the scripture: "**The way of man is forward and strange: but as for the pure, his work is right.**" The New International Version puts it this way: "**The way of the guilty is devious, but the conduct of the innocent is upright**" (Proverbs 21:8).

Start defeating your secret agent mentality exactly where the battle is taking place: in your mind.

- Realize everyone is not out to get you.
- Make a list of all the nice things people have done for you (Philippians 4:8).
- Make a second list of your desires for your home.
- Break out of your shell. Make appointments with the experts who can help you obtain your desire for a home.
- Ascertain just how much has been added to you by spending time acknowledging just how much you have grown.

Once you actually schedule appointments and meet with your reliable real estate agent and mortgage lender, surely you will discover professional, well-informed persons available to help you. Since you are simply gathering information, do not sign anything until you are sure you are ready to begin formally applying for a mortgage. Even then, be sure you read everything in **all** documents before you sign. If there is something you do not understand, ask questions. Rely on the experts, remembering that the secret agent mentality has been laid to rest.

Undoubtedly, you will actually enjoy talking to individuals whose sole focus is to help you achieve your goal of home ownership. A reliable professional should have no problem with you knowing your rights.

Remember this: The real estate agent, mortgage loan officer, and closing attorney do not get paid if you do not purchase a home. If by chance you are displeased with the service, the ball is in your court. Let supervisors know (in writing) the reasons for your dissatisfaction. If the problem is not solved, find someone else to work with you and for you in your quest of home ownership. Just make sure you do not crawl back into your secret agent cave.

# Defeating *Giant* Number 6 – Mr. and Ms. Know It All

No one knows everything, and that includes you. Your inability to ask questions and to listen to others keeps you talking more than you listen. It is okay to ask questions! When you do, just make sure you are obtaining your information from the right source, from individuals who are skilled in the area of information you seek.

You may think that great sums of money are required to obtain a home mortgage. In today's market, it is not necessarily true that having great sums of money is a must to obtain a home of your own.

Please hear me. There is a right and wrong way to do just about anything. Having a know-it-all attitude may be what is keeping you from occupying your promise. If you heard it through the grapevine, more than likely the information is not entirely accurate.

Only insecure people have a problem with enjoying the accomplishments and intellect of others. Therefore, you should avoid walking in insecurity and the know-it-all attitude. Instead, make efforts to celebrate and acknowledge the wonderful things about the many wonderful people you encounter. The more you practice this type of "right" attitude, the easier it will be to walk in it.

Make a kind, humble nature your habitual state. In doing so, you slay the "Know It All" *giant*, now feeding a wholesome and sincere nature. You do not have to be a farmer to understand the principle of sowing and reaping. Treat others as you wish to be treated.

> "And ye shall know that truth, and the truth shall make you free" (John 8:32).

## Defeating *Giant* Number 7 – Bankruptcy

Look now at two types of bankruptcy, Chapter 13 and Chapter 7. Because you were ill informed, you believed that bankruptcy was the end. You feared dreaming of owning your own home. Thoughts of never being able to obtain an approved mortgage loan and demand the best interest rates have plagued you.

The "Bankruptcy" *giant* has tyrannized many. However, with the right information, this *giant*, too, can be reckoned with. See the chart on the next page for understanding the steps to bankruptcy.

**Prior to filing bankruptcy and for a complete understanding of the process, be sure to consult with a bankruptcy attorney.**

```
┌─────────────────────────────────┐
│   Looking to file bankruptcy    │
└─────────────────────────────────┘
                 ↓
┌─────────────────────────────────┐
│  Participate in an approved Credit │
│  Counseling Program within 6    │
│  months before you file bankruptcy. │
└─────────────────────────────────┘
                 ↓
┌─────────────────────────────────┐
│  Is your current monthly income │
│  higher than the average income │
│       level in the state?       │
└─────────────────────────────────┘
```

**Yes** ↔ **No**

↓          ↓
↓     ┌ ─ ─ ─ ─ ─ ─ ─ ─ ─ ─ ─ ┐
↓     :   **Can file Chapter 7**   :
↓     └ ─ ─ ─ ─ ─ ─ ─ ─ ─ ─ ─ ┘

```
┌─────────────────────────────────┐        ↑
│          Net Income =           │        ↑
│ (Current Monthly Income – Monthly Expenses) x 60 │  ↑ No
│                                 │        ↑
└─────────────────────────────────┘        ↑
```

                 ↓

┌───────────────────────────────────────────────────┐
│ **Is Net Income > $9,999 or > 25% of Unsecured Debt?** │
└───────────────────────────────────────────────────┘

                 ↓

┌ ─ ─ ─ ─ ─ ─ ─ ─ ─ ─ ─ ─ ─ ┐
:      **Can file Chapter 13**      :
└ ─ ─ ─ ─ ─ ─ ─ ─ ─ ─ ─ ─ ─ ┘

## Chapter 13 Bankruptcy

Did you know that if you are a year or two into bankruptcy, the "trustee" of your bankruptcy has the authority to "okay" you to purchase property? This is why it is imperative that you honor the agreement that you established in the bankruptcy. There may be lending institutions that will forego the mandatory one to two year waiting period after the discharge date and grant you a loan.

If you are completely discharged from your bankruptcy, in as recent as 24 hours, you may be able to obtain a mortgage loan (provided your credit is now acceptable). This can occur after bankruptcy if you have established a minimum of three to five positive credit ratings and met all other mortgage loan requirements.

## Chapter 7 Bankruptcy

If you are in a Chapter 7 Bankruptcy and there was no property involved, there is good news. You do not have to wait an entire seven years before obtaining a mortgage! In as little as two years after your discharge date, you can obtain a mortgage loan.

However, if your Chapter 7 Bankruptcy included foreclosed property, the waiting period is three years after the discharge date in many instances. Yet, there is an end to the waiting.

**To defeat the "Bankruptcy"** *giant,* **it is important that you reestablish positive credit.** After any type of bankruptcy, establishing positive credit is paramount. In some instances lenders will utilize what is called alternate credit. Trade lines such as your rental history, utility payment history, automobile insurance, and even your cellular phone payments may be utilized (if they demonstrate an excellent payment history over at least the most recent twelve months). You should be aware that the lender will scrutinize your credit record closely because of the bankruptcy, and such non-traditional methods, while possible, are less likely to be utilized.

As previously stated, opening a secured loan or adding your name to a family member's already excellently established account is a great way to establish new credit! (You can ask any banker how to obtain a secured loan.) Please understand and realize this: What appears to be the worst of situations does not necessarily have to be an impossible or permanent situation!

### Consumer Credit Counseling

If you are undergoing Consumer Credit Counseling, please see the explanation under Chapter 13 Bankruptcy. The same rules **usually** apply.

When seeking financial restoration after bankruptcy, begin by making a list of all your debts. Next, arrange the debts according to amounts owed, from least to the highest. Focus on paying off the smallest bills first by making sure you, of course, pay all your obligations each month.

Once you have eliminated your smaller bills, use this extra cash to tackle your larger bills. A reliable financial planner may assist you in establishing a workable budget. He or she will be able to help you strategize on the best way to tackle your finances.

**Faithfulness and consistently honoring your debts with timely payments can right most serious credit concerns.** If you have more than one credit card, you may be able to transfer balances from the high interest cards to the credit card with the lowest interest rate. When consolidating your debt in this way, competing credit card companies may even offer to lower your interest rate to retain your business. It is not unlikely that a type of bidding war may result, in an effort to keep you from leaving their company.

If you face additional obstacles—corporate prejudice, fear of rejection, fear of the required paperwork, generational curses of poverty, or other unnamed barriers—believe in your heart that these, too, can be conquered.

Please know this: The lending institution is not in business to turn you down! They want you to be able to obtain a home loan because this is one of the ways they make their money.

**If you are unpleasantly or unfairly treated, please remember that there is more than**

**one bank and loan officer. Even with the worst credit history or smallest of mortgage loans, you have the right to be treated with courtesy and respect!**

Far too often many individuals fall prey to the past, believing that because no one in their family accomplished a particular thing, neither can they. Please understand that you are an individual, equipped by God with your own set of strengths. You are God's creation, and He has not set you up for failure.

Do you believe Genesis 1:26? Can you believe that you are an individual who has been wonderfully created and that there is no one else quite like you?

> "I will praise thee; for I am fearfully and wonderfully made: marvelous are thy works; and that my soul knoweth right well" (Psalm 139:14).

You are special! You are important! You have an inheritance! If you can believe this truth, then you are on your way to defeating this obstacle as well! The actions of your mother, grandfather, third cousin, uncle so-and-so, or other family members do not have to dictate your present and future! Do not allow the failures of your relatives to become the excuse or permanent script in your life. Realize your inheritance!

"The heaven, even the heavens, are the Lord's: but the earth hath he given to the children of men" (Psalm 115:16).

# Use the space below to decree which giants will fall forever defeated in your life.

_____

_____

_____

_____

_____

_____

_____

_____

_____

_____

_____

_____

_____

_____

"Thou shalt also decree a thing, and it shall be established unto thee; and the light shall shine upon thy ways" (Job 22:28).

## Chapter Four

# DOCUMENTATION IS REQUIRED

Do not become anxious about the thorough scrutiny the mortgage company will employ to examine your financial standing. Understand that this is a part of the process.

The next page lists information that the mortgage company may request when you apply for a home loan. Place a check next to the items that are applicable to you. When you visit your loan officer, be sure you bring those checked items.

- [ ] A copy of your most recent income tax returns
- [ ] W2 forms for the last two years
- [ ] 1099 forms for the last three years
- [ ] Your most recent pay stubs (in the last two months)
- [ ] Your landlord's name, address and phone number for past two years
- [ ] The name and address of your employer (in the past two years)
- [ ] Account numbers for all checking, savings, and investment accounts
- [ ] Information on all credit cards
- [ ] Loan documents on other real estate owned, including lender address and loan number
- [ ] Estimated value of furniture and personal property
- [ ] Certificate of eligibility (CDs)
- [ ] DD214's (military persons only)
- [ ] Name, address, and phone number of nearest relatives
- [ ] Money for an official credit application ($60.00 to $90.00)
- [ ] Driver's license (or state identification card) and social security card
- [ ] Copy(s) of official divorce decree (if applicable)
- [ ] Copy of bankruptcy and discharge papers
- [ ] Copy of insurance policies
- [ ] If self-employed, see your loan officer for special requirements.

These documents are used to gain a thorough and accurate profile of your financial capabilities. Your lender will use the information to decide your credit worthiness and financial stability, in order to "prequalify" you for a home loan.

At the moment, you may not have a two-year work history. You may have only worked for the past year. You now know that in most cases the lending institution is looking for a minimum of a two-year work history. However, there are situations when the lending institution will ignore the two years of work requirement. For example, if you are a recent graduate and have obtained permanent employment in your field of study, lenders may forego the traditional two-year work requirement.

Ideally, all past due debts should be paid before you close on your homeowner's loan. Some lending institutions, however, will allow you to provide proof of past due debts being paid off by bringing receipts as recent as ten days before the date you close on your home.

Most lending institutions do want to see that you have paid your current debt on time for the last twelve months.

Remember, you do not necessarily need a flawless credit record. The important thing to realize is that the lending institution is looking for evidence of stability, a consistent record of you having paid the debt you already have. You will also need to demonstrate your ability to repay the mortgage loan you are seeking. If your income is stretched to its limits, this will be impossible to demonstrate.

If the mortgage officer and real estate professionals are knowledgeable and deserve your business, they will gladly answer your questions. Be fair by remembering that you are not the person's only client. Scheduling an appointment is, therefore, a good idea.

Equally important is bringing to your scheduled meetings the required documents and a prepared list of your concerns and questions. By doing this, you will be able to avoid making numerous phone calls to your loan officer or real estate agent, which may often result in frustration because he or she may not be available at your beck and call. **It is highly likely that your questions may not receive their needed attention until everything can be addressed in your <u>scheduled appointments</u>.**

It is not my intent to be laborious or technical in this book so for a more detailed explanation on the mortgage loan process, please see a reputable loan officer.

It is my hope that being aware of required documentation will help you feel less intimidated and more prepared for the mortgage application process.

# Three Basic Areas of Mortgage Qualification

## 1. EMPLOYMENT
Self-Employed
- A minimum three year work history
- 1099s (most recent three years)
- Income tax returns (most recent three years)

Employee
- Minimum two years work history
- W2s (two years)
- Income Tax Returns (two years)

Graduate
- A recent school certificate or college degree(s) may be used in lieu of work record
- Obtained permanent employment
- Verifiable with employer

## 2. DEBT-TO-INCOME
- Must meet pre-established ratio
- Only **long-term** debt considered
- Some medical debts may be ignored

## 3. CREDIT HISTORY
- All revolving accounts (in last 12 months) must show debt has been paid on time
- All delinquencies (also known as "charge offs") must be paid off to a zero balance
- Evidence of payment must be reflected by a zero balance in all reporting credit bureaus
- No new revolving accounts opened a minimum of 60 to 180 days prior to closing

You can do it! You can become a homeowner. Your clear mind, coupled with patience, will see you through to success. Now it is time to gather all the paperwork you need to put you one step closer to owning your own home.

Be sure to ask your loan officer for details concerning the information listed on the previous page.

# Use the space below to write your specific questions about qualifying for a mortgage.

_____

_____

_____

_____

_____

_____

_____

_____

_____

_____

_____

_____

_____

"...and with all getting, get an understanding" (Proverbs 4:7).

## Chapter Five

# WHICH MOUNTAIN IS YOURS?

Of course, almost everyone wants the most fabulous, fantastic, gorgeous, and largest of homes. However, everyone cannot afford such a property. This is a great time to point you to another scripture and speak on a beautiful Bible truth. It is my hope that this scripture will give you wisdom in selecting and purchasing the appropriate home.

James 4:3 states: **"Ye ask, and receive not, because ye ask amiss, that ye may consume it upon your lusts."**

This scripture and entire book of James is credited as being authored by James, the natural brother of Jesus Christ. The entire theme of James concerns good works. In other words, perform works or deeds that are good because of the *motive*, not merely the surface appearance.

**Do not fall into the trap of trying to buy a particular home to impress others.** God indeed wants you to be prosperous. He wants you to be blessed. Our blessings, however, are often directly in proportion to our preparedness and our proven demonstration of responsible stewardship.

If you have not been faithful over few or little things, you may not be ready for the huge things. Maybe you have been faithful, but financially it is not realistic to buy at the top of your qualifying limit. After all, the mortgage is not the only monthly expense you will incur.

**Every potential homebuyer can avoid unnecessary frustration by adhering to the points on the following two pages.**

1. When looking at property, have a written list of your major desires for your home.

2. Be sure to consider the cost of the house (and the loan amount for which you qualified) when you prepare your wish list. Champagne taste with ginger ale money will only frustrate you—so be realistic.

3. Do not try to purchase a property to please or impress others. If you are satisfied with it, no one else's opinion is more important. You, after all, are the one who is responsible for paying the debt.

4. When selecting your home, be sure to consider all the important factors to you and your family, such as safety and appearance of the neighborhood, proximity to work and schools, and location of amenities such as shops and grocery stores.

5. Be realistic by realizing that if you are not building the home, you may not find a house that perfectly matches your wish list. You may have to do small things such as change a room's color, take down wallpaper, settle for a smaller kitchen because you opted for larger bedrooms, etc.

6. Be sure to look at the house in the daylight hours.

7. Take notes on each property showing. After looking at more than two or three properties, you may begin to forget the details of each of the houses. (See "Renee's Inventory Forms for House Hunting" in Give Me This Mountain: The Workbook Version.)

8. Drive by the property on weekends and at night so that you can evaluate the amount of noise and "hanging out" in the neighborhood.

9. Try to notify your Realtor at least 24 hours prior to the day you want to house hunt. Courtesy is always a good idea.

10. Avoid obtaining information from people who are not professionally trained or experienced in the area of mortgage loans, real estate, building construction, etc. This source of information may not be accurate and may serve to only frustrate or alarm you unnecessarily.

11. Ask questions. Do not be ashamed if you do not know what may seem to be the simplest of things. Since buying property is serious business and often involves prolonged debt, you have the right to be treated with patience and honesty. At the same time, remember to be reasonable in your expectations. No *one* person knows everything!

12. **Avoid wasting time looking in an area that you really do not desire, and at a price point that you cannot afford.** While you are looking "just out of curiosity," someone else may be writing a purchase offer on the house that would have fit you (and your budget) perfectly.

As you view properties, be sure you focus on the property itself, and not the current owner's décor. With these invaluable tips, you can utilize your time efficiently in finding the property that is satisfying to you and your family.

You have defeated your credit and money *giants*, saved the necessary funds, submitted the required documents, prequalified for a home loan, and identified the house that will best fit you and your budget.

**Now it is time to *Go Get Your Mountain*!**

# Use the space below to write the tips from this book that are especially vital to you.

_____

_____

_____

_____

_____

_____

_____

_____

_____

_____

_____

_____

_____

_____

"And beside this, giving all diligence, add to your faith virtue; and to virtue knowledge..." (2 Peter 1:5).

## Chapter Six
# GO GET YOUR MOUNTAIN!

You have done it! You are an overcomer, having broken through chains that once bound you! You have defeated the *giants* that stood between you and property ownership. With the help of a real estate agent, you are now ready to make a formal offer on a house.

At this point in the process, make sure that you:

- Know the interest rate of the loan. If it is not "locked" and in writing, it does not exist.
- Understand whether the interest rate is fixed or adjustable.

- Ask the lender for a Good Faith Estimate. (This is a document that provides the estimated monthly mortgage payment and the anticipated dollars you will need to close on the property.)
- Verify that there is no prepayment penalty on the loan (in case you want to make extra payments).

I will be brief in this chapter. My main goal, after all, was to get you to this point. Your real estate agent will be able to provide you with the correct forms, explain all forms in detail, and walk you through each step in your home ownership journey. He or she should be available for you throughout the entire process.

This includes:

- Making your offer to purchase
- Obtaining an accepted contract
- Aiding you in selecting a licensed home inspector
- Assisting you in acquiring quotes for home an hazard insurance
- Scheduling your final walkthrough
- Attending your very own closing where you sign on the dotted line and become a property owner

The list on the next page is an example of some of the forms that may be used to purchase your property.

1. Agreement to Purchase and Sell: This is the form used to make and accept the written offer on the property. When submitting this offer, a monetary deposit is normally necessary to accompany the offer, or all parties involved should submit it immediately upon agreement to a contract.

2. Agency Disclosure: This form, once completed, discloses to the buyer and seller exactly who the real estate agent is working for.

3. Property Condition Disclosure: This document provides important information about the property you are about to purchase. It will disclose information such as age of the property, roof, appliances, heating and cooling systems, etc. This paperwork also discloses whether the property has ever flooded or been damaged by fire or termites. The Property Condition Disclosure should be presented to you within 24 hours of a signed purchase agreement between a buyer and a seller. A buyer has 72 hours to return this form signed. Otherwise, the contract can be considered null and void.

4. Lead Based Disclosure: A Lead Based Disclosure and Lead Based Booklet must be presented to all property buyers purchasing a property that was built in 1978 or before. This booklet provides what could be life-saving information about the use of lead-based paint. A buyer signing this form attests that they are aware that lead-based paint may exist. Usually, this is not a reason to fear buying such a property. Since approximately 1978, lead ceased to be utilized in paint.

For other types of purchases such as HUD, VA, and Vacant Land, there may be additions or variations in the forms utilized. Your professionally licensed Realtor will be informed and equipped with all the necessary paperwork. Just remember this: You have nothing to fear.

> "For God hath not given us the spirit of fear; but of power, and of love, and of a sound mind" (2 Timothy 1:7).

While home ownership is a big responsibility, you know who you are, and you no longer allow obstacles to defeat you. You have tackled them all! When and if you should get nervous about the responsibilities, just tell yourself: "I am as capable and competent as anyone else." Then make sure you stick to your sensible budget. If others can do it, so can you.

You are, after all, God's unique creation. He delights in you. You are His child. You have Him to thank for getting your mountain!

## Chapter Seven

# MAINTAINING YOUR MOUNTAIN

You are now among the millions of blessed people who own property! Congratulations!

The purchase of a home is perhaps the single largest debt you will ever incur. Should you decide to sell your property for a second, third, fourth or even fifth purchase, its condition will be of great importance to you when it comes to resale value and equity.

**Your property is a valuable possession, but a poorly maintained property will adversely affect this value. Take care of your home. Keep it neat and clean. Be sure to stay abreast of the required maintenance.** This is vital because your property, if properly cared for, will in most instances increase in value, providing you equity.

It is also important to have balance. While you may truly love your home, do not mistakenly improve it beyond the value of other homes in the neighborhood. In such instances you will have what is called a "white elephant." (The official term for "white elephant" is *diminishing return*.) Your home, no matter how wonderful, is only worth the neighborhood in which it sits.

It is not enough to own the property. You also need to make certain you do not lose the property. Remember that you worked hard to obtain your own home, so be sure to pay all mortgage and other expenses in a timely fashion.

If you ever face financial difficulty, you may need to borrow some or all of the equity in your home to prevent poor credit or loss of the property. **As a property owner, under certain conditions, you can borrow against your own property's equity for just about any reason** (e.g., home improvement, college money for children, wedding costs, vacations, etc.).

Before allowing yourself to fall behind in your mortgage payments and lose your home, obtaining an equity loan may be the answer. It is important in such instances not to wait until you have fallen so far behind that your credit standing will not allow you to be approved for an equity loan. Do not wait until the bank has decided to foreclose on your home.

If you find yourself in the predicament of needing money to prevent the loss of the very home you worked so hard to obtain, do not panic or proceed in denial. Act by contacting your loan officer, real estate agent, or persons at the company that own your mortgage. Remember, you have faced your *giants* in the past, and you can continue to defeat them should new situations arise. For further guidance after your home purchase, a real estate agent is waiting to assist you!

I will end this book as I began it, by reminding you that you were created with both purpose and plan. In order to achieve your goals, they, too, will be realized when you live your life with purpose and according to a plan. Do not, however, assume that even then every step will be smooth and that life will proceed without struggle.

Ecclesiastes 9:11 declares:

> "I returned, and saw under the sun, that the race is not to the swift, nor the battle to the strong, neither yet bread to the wise, nor yet riches to men of understanding, nor yet favour to men of skill, but time and chance happeneth to them all."

Yet, press on you must, for as you believe, you will achieve!

# Renee's Sack of House Hunting Tools

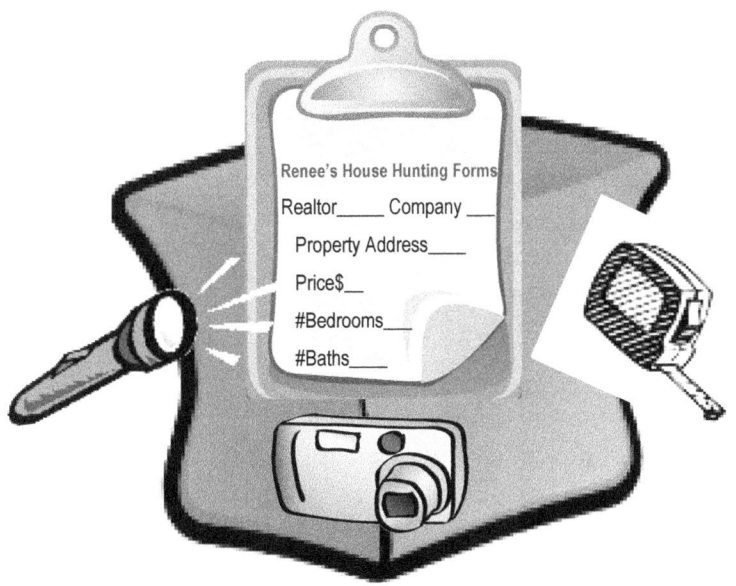

Be sure you bring along "Renee's Inventory Forms for House Hunting" (See Give Me This Mountain: The Working Book Version):

1. Tape measure: A tape measure can be helpful, should you need to obtain measurements of windows or doorways. If you have large furniture or a sectional sofa, it is possible that you may have difficulty getting such items into the home. Measure twice for safety and the elimination of potential frustration.

2. Flash light(s): You may find yourself viewing properties that have no electricity. In such cases, it may be difficult to see certain rooms well. Having a large bright flashlight will solve this problem.

3. Small ball or marble: If the floor feels unlevel, placing a marble or ball in the center of the floor is a great way to determine if it is at an angle. If the ball or marble rolls, then it is highly likely that the floor is unlevel. You will, of course, point this concern out to your home inspector for verification.

4. Camera: Taking pictures is a great way to look back on your favorite properties and recall particular features.

5. List of Must-Haves: Looking with clear focus is aided when you compare any home you view with your very own list of "must haves" you have prepared. You have made this wish list with a clear understanding of your price range and the types of amenities available in this price range.

6. Another pair of eyes: Another pair of eyes is very helpful in identifying both the positives and negatives of the properties you view. Family members and close friends can be a great source of enthusiasm and can sometimes provide much needed objectivity.

# U.S. CONSTITUTION: FIFTH AMENDMENT

## The Constitution

**We the People** of the United States, in Order to form a more perfect Union, establish Justice, insure domestic Tranquility, provide for the common Defence, promote the general Welfare, and secure the Blessings of Liberty to ourselves and our Posterity, do ordain and establish this CONSTITUTION for the United States of America.

### Article. I.

SECTION. 1. All legislative Powers herein granted shall be vested in a Congress of the United States, which shall consist of a Senate and House of Representatives.

SECTION. 2. The House of Representatives shall be composed of Members chosen every second Year by the People of the several States, and the Electors in each State shall have the Qualifications requisite for Electors of the most numerous Branch of the State Legislature.

No Person shall be a Representative who shall not have attained to the Age of twenty-five Years, and been seven Years a Citizen of the United States, and who shall not, when elected, be an Inhabitant of that State in which he shall be chosen.

[Representatives and direct Taxes shall be apportioned among the several States which may be included within this Union, according to their respective Numbers, which shall be determined by adding to the whole Number of free Persons, including those bound to Service for a Term of Years, and excluding Indians not taxed, three fifths of all other Persons.] The actual Enumeration shall be made within three Years after the first Meeting of the Congress of the United States, and within every subsequent Term of ten Years, in such Manner as they shall by Law direct. The Number of Representatives shall not exceed one for every thirty Thousand, but each State shall have at Least one Representative; and until such enumeration shall be made, the State of New Hampshire shall be entitled to chuse three, Massachusetts eight, Rhode-Island and Providence Plantations one, Connecticut five, New-York six, New Jersey four, Pennsylvania eight, Delaware one, Maryland six, Virginia ten, North Carolina five, South Carolina five, and Georgia three.

When vacancies happen in the Representation from any State, the Executive Authority thereof shall issue Writs of Election to fill such Vacancies.

The House of Representatives shall chuse their Speaker and other Officers; and shall have the sole Power of Impeachment.

SECTION. 3. The Senate of the United States shall be composed of two Senators from each State, chosen by the Legislature thereof, for six Years; and each Senator shall have one Vote.

Immediately after they shall be assembled in Consequence of the first Election, they shall be divided as equally as may be into three Classes. The Seats of the Senators of the first Class shall be vacated at the Expiration of the second Year, of the second Class at the Expiration of the fourth Year, and of the third Class at the Expiration of the sixth Year, so that one-third may be chosen every second Year; and if Vacancies happen by Resignation, or otherwise, during the Recess of the Legislature of any State, the Executive thereof may make temporary Appointments until the next Meeting of the Legislature, which shall then fill such Vacancies.

No Person shall be a Senator who shall not have attained to the Age of thirty Years, and been nine Years a Citizen of the United States, and who shall not, when elected, be an Inhabitant of that State for which he shall be chosen.

The Vice President of the United States shall be President of the Senate, but shall have no Vote, unless they be equally divided.

The Senate shall chuse their other Officers, and also a President pro tempore, in the Absence of the Vice President, or when he shall exercise the Office of President of the United States.

The Senate shall have the sole Power to try all Impeachments. When sitting for that Purpose, they shall be on Oath or Affirmation. When the President of the United States is tried, the Chief Justice shall preside: And no Person shall be convicted without the Concurrence of two thirds of the Members present.

Judgment in Cases of Impeachment shall not extend further than to removal from Office, and disqualification to hold and enjoy any Office of honor, Trust or Profit under the United States: but the Party convicted shall nevertheless be liable and subject to Indictment, Trial, Judgment and Punishment, according to Law.

## U.S. Constitution: Fifth Amendment

### Fifth Amendment - Rights of Persons

No person shall be held to answer for a capital, or otherwise infamous crime, unless on a presentment or indictment of a Grand Jury, except in cases arising in the land or naval forces, or in the Militia, when in actual service in time of War or public danger; nor shall any person be subject for the same offence to be twice put in jeopardy of life or limb; nor shall be compelled in any criminal case to be a witness against himself, nor be deprived of life, liberty, or property, without due process of law; nor shall private property be taken for public use, without just compensation.

# References

- Holy Bible, King James Version
- Holy Bible, New International Version
- Vines Bible Dictionary
- Webster Dictionary
- Constitution of the United States of America - The Fifth Amendment of the Bill of Rights
- Freedom Edition of American Civics by Hartley Vincent

# TERMS TO KNOW AND UNDERSTAND

## 1. appraisal –

- An estimate of value, as for sale, assessment, or taxation; valuation
- The decided/accepted value of a property
- (Currently in some states, an "official" appraisal is good for six months on a given property.)

## 2. closing/real estate closing –

- An official meeting in which a buyer, seller, real estate attorney, and/or real estate agent(s) normally attend, where the real estate attorney presents the official documents to transfer the deed/title from the sellers to the purchaser
- (Currently in some states, it is the standard/common practice that the purchaser does not occupy the property until it is "closed.")

## 3. deposit –

- To give as security or in part payment
- Money that is attached to a contract offer as part of payment of the balance of funds due
- (Sometimes the terms deposit and earnest money are used interchangeably. However they are not necessarily the same in terms of the rules/real estate laws that govern them. Talk to your real estate agent to learn the difference.)

## 4. earnest money –

- Money given by a buyer to a seller to bind a contract
- Money that is supplied to show serious intent when an offer is made to purchase real estate
- (Sometimes the terms deposit and earnest money are used interchangeably. However they are not necessarily the same in terms of the rules/real estate laws that govern them. Talk to your real estate agent to learn the difference. *When you are working with a real estate agent/company, the earnest money is not given directly to the seller of the home. Instead, the listing company's broker holds the money in a non-interest bearing account.)

## 5. equity –

- The monetary value of a property or business beyond any amounts owed on it in mortgages, claims, liens, etc.
- (Example: A property is valued at $100,000, but the principal owed is $80,000 and no other liens are attached to the property. The owner of the property then has $20,000 in equity.)

## 6. escrow –

- State of a deed held until conditions are met
- (Example: The mortgage company may require a certain amount of funds to be collected from a buyer and hold these funds in an escrow account to be sure any possible shortages of taxes, insurances, etc. are covered.)

# 7. home inspection –

- The act of observing/analyzing the state of a property or specific areas of a property
- (Once a contract to purchase is established, be sure you hire a licensed inspector, who will give you a written report concerning the condition of specific areas of the property, i.e. roof, A/C unit, furnace, etc.)

# 8. real estate agent –

- A person who is licensed in a given state to assist buyers and sellers in the sale or purchase of (real) property.
- Also called a Licensee

# 9. REALTOR –

- A licensed real estate agent who pays a sum of money to be a member of a local/state/national board that gives the agent access to the real estate information within a given area through a Multi-Listing Service (MLS)
- REALTORS are held to a strict code of ethics.
- (Usually a REALTOR has access to the sold or current for sale properties in a particular city, area, or parish/county, along with other valuable information.)

# About the Author

Renee Yvonne McGee Whitley is a Louisiana Licensed REALTOR. A native of Chicago, Illinois, she has spent the majority of her years as a resident of the South. The youngest of ten children, she learned early how to be heard. She has a twin sister and is the mother of four children. Her family circle is a large one, as she is also a stepmother and grandmother. A believer of God and in people, she focuses her work toward "ministering" to others. Renee confesses to be deeply in love with one very special man, stating that being "found" by her husband, William, was one of the best things to happen in her life.

In her own words, Renee says: "I found that there were so many people who thought the idea of property ownership was only for those with perfect credit or for those who had a lot of money. I was astonished when I encountered so many people who were actually afraid to even attempt to buy property for fear of being turned down, and this hurt me. Because of this, I decided to do two things that I believe were inspired by God: (1) treat each client that I am privileged to serve with patience and respect, regardless of the amount of money they are spending, despite how long it may take to service them; and (2) educate my clients to the best of my ability to broaden their possibilities for home ownership."

Renee credits a broker, Juan Bolden, for motivating her to pursue the real estate track. However, this is not her only area of expertise. She is also a Speech Language Pathologist, Minister of the Gospel, and poet. Renee confesses a love for all types of music, people, and places. It is her desire that this book truly provide you with some understanding, as well as inspiration, in your quest to home ownership.

A rare "bird" in this day and age, when you read her writings, you will no doubt see that her wings have taken flight.

Written by Paulette Lucille Grey

# UPCOMING PROJECTS

by

# RENEE MCGEE WHITLEY

## GIVE ME THIS MOUNTAIN:
*The Working Book Version*


## RENEE'S HOUSE HUNTING FORMS


## MR. & MRS. SUNFLOWER
*Children's Book Series*


The author is available for seminars, conferences, and real estate consultations.

To contact Renee McGee Whitley
or for more information, visit:

## www.writerenee.com